Breakthrough Inventions

INVENTING THE PRINTING PRESS

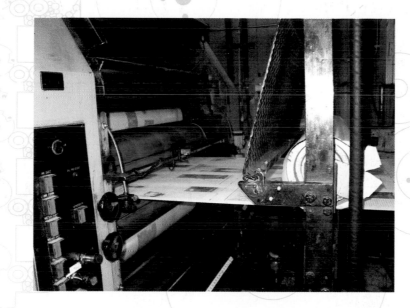

Lisa Mullins

Crabtree Publishing Company

www.crabtreebooks.com

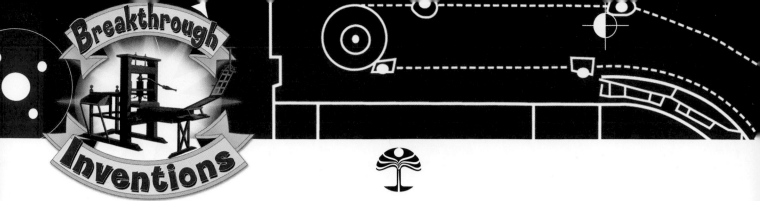

Crabtree Publishing Company
www.crabtreebooks.com

Coordinating editor: Ellen Rodger

Series and project editor: Adrianna Morganelli

Designer and production coordinator: Rosie Gowsell

Production assistant: Samara Parent

Art director: Rob MacGregor

Prepress technician: Nancy Johnson

Project development, editing, photo editing, and layout: First Folio Resource Group, Inc.: Tom Dart, Sarah Gleadow, Debbie Smith

Photo research: Maria DeCambra, Linda Tanaka

Consultants: Mark Barbour, Curator, The International Printing Museum, Carson, CA; Dr. Todd Samuelson, Curator, The Museum of Printing History; Constance Simms, St. Mary's Junior School, Cambridge; Nicholas Smith, Cambridge University Library

Photographs: akg-images: p. 22 (left); Paul Almasy/Corbis: p. 27 (left); AP Photo/Keystone/Martial Trezzini: p. 31 (top); Art Archive/Museo del Prado Madrid/Dagli Orti: p. 15 (left); Bettmann/Corbis: p. 7 (left), p. 16, p. 17 (bottom), p. 19; Bibliothèque des Arts Décoratifs, Paris, France/Archives Charmet/Bridgeman Art Library: p. 12; Bibliothèque Nationale, Paris, France/Bridgeman Art Library: p. 7 (right); Bildarchiv Preussischer Kulturbesitz/Art Resource, NY: p. 8; British Library/C.108.d.35 front cover: p. 11 (left); British Library/G.9382 f.1: p. 11 (right); British Library, London, UK/© British Library Board. All Rights Reserved/Bridgeman Art Library: p. 6; British Museum, London, UK/Bridgeman Art Library: p. 4 (bottom);

Michael Donne/Science Photo Library: p. 22 (right); Giraudon/Art Resource, NY: p. 13 (left); Granger Collection, New York: title page (top), copyright page, p. 5 (top), p. 9 (bottom), p. 14, p. 18, p. 23 (right); International Printing Museum: cover (right); iStockphoto.com/Jim Mires Photography: p. 29 (left); iStockphoto.com/Ariusz Nawrocki: contents page; Lester Lefkowitz/Corbis: p. 30; Louvre, Paris, France/Bridgeman Art Library: p. 4 (top); Mary Evans Picture Library: p. 10; The Museum of Printing History: p. 9 (top); Reuters/Corbis: p. 27 (right); Scala/Art Resource, NY: p. 5 (bottom); Science Museum, London, UK/Bridgeman Art Library: p. 17 (top); Ellen Rodger: title page (bottom), p. 25 (top), p. 26; Science Museum Library/Science & Society Picture Library: p. 15 (right); Telecommunications History Group: p. 29 (right); Victoria & Albert Museum, London/Art Resource, NY: p. 13 (right), p. 28 (bottom); Courtesy of Xerox Corporation: p. 25 (bottom); Other images from stock CD.

Cover: Over the last 400 years, printing presses have undergone many changes. Large, wooden presses, which required a lot of strength to operate, have been replaced by modern presses that are controlled almost entirely by computers.

Title page: Presses print color books in four separate layers: cyan, which is blue; magenta, which is red; yellow; and black.

Contents page: Early printing presses used individual pieces of metal type to print letters, numbers, and punctuation. The characters on each piece of type were formed backward so that they would print the correct way on the page.

Library and Archives Canada Cataloguing in Publication

Mullins, Lisa, 1981-
    Inventing the Printing Press / Lisa Mullins.

(Breakthrough Inventions)
Includes index.
ISBN 978-0-7787-2819-1 (bound)
ISBN 978-0-7787-2841-2 (pbk.)

    1. Printing presses--History--Juvenile literature.
2. Inventions--Juvenile literature. I. Title. II. Series.

Z124.M64 2007   j686.2   C2007-900667-1

Library of Congress Cataloging-in-Publication Data

Mullins, Lisa, 1981-
    Inventing the Printing Press / written by Lisa Mullins.
        p. cm. -- (Breakthrough Inventions)
    Includes index.
    ISBN-13: 978-0-7787-2819-1 (rlb)
    ISBN-10: 0-7787-2819-6 (rlb)
    ISBN-13: 978-0-7787-2841-2 (pb)
    ISBN-10: 0-7787-2841-2 (pb)
    1. Printing--History--Juvenile literature. 2. Printing presses--History--Juvenile literature. I. Title. II. Series.

Z124.M935 2007
686.2--dc22   2007002923
                                                         LC

Crabtree Publishing Company

www.crabtreebooks.com   1-800-387-7650

Published in Canada
Crabtree Publishing
616 Welland Ave.
St. Catharines, Ontario
L2M 5V6

Published in the United States
Crabtree Publishing
PMB16A
350 Fifth Ave., Suite 3308
New York, NY 10118

Published in the United Kingdom
Crabtree Publishing
White Cross Mills
High Town, Lancaster
LA1 4XS

Published in Australia
Crabtree Publishing
386 Mt. Alexander Rd.
Ascot Vale (Melbourne)
VIC 3032

Contents
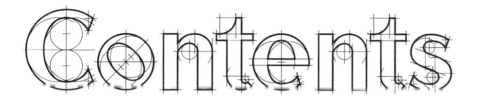

Written Words

Without the printing press, books such as this one would not exist. The printing press is a machine that produces many copies of books, newspapers, magazines, and other printed materials very quickly. Before the printing press was invented, every single text was made by hand, which required a lot of time and concentration.

Tablets

The first system of writing, called cuneiform, was invented around 3000 B.C. by the ancient peoples of Mesopotamia, an area in present-day Iraq. Cuneiform used simple pictures combined with lines to form words and phrases. Writers used a **stylus** to carve the pictures and lines into a piece of soft clay. The clay was then dried in the sun or baked in a stone oven until it was hard.

Cuneiform tablets were mostly used as records of items that were traded, and for government documents.

Scrolls

By 3000 B.C., the Egyptians were preserving texts and images on papyrus scrolls. Papyrus is a tall plant that grows along the Nile River. When it is cut into strips, hammered flat, and dried, it can be used like paper. **Scribes** wrote on papyrus using brushes and pens made of thick reeds, and ink made from plants and **soot**. They recorded prayers for the dead, descriptions of religious ceremonies, and observations of the stars and planets. To make a book, scribes glued the ends of papyrus sheets together, rolled the glued sheets into scrolls, and fastened them with bits of leather, cord, cloth, or string.

Papyrus scrolls have been discovered inside the tombs of important people, such as royalty and priests.

Medieval Codices

By 100 A.D., a new form of text called a codex was being used in Europe. Codices, which originated in Egypt, are texts with pages that are folded and bound together on one side, like this book. Codices were smaller than scrolls, which made them easier to carry around, and the wooden covers of codices protected the pages inside. Codices were also more convenient to read because they could be easily opened to any page, unlike scrolls, which had to be unrolled to the correct section of text.

Codices were first used by governments to keep records. In the early **Middle Ages**, codices were written by hand and were usually called manuscripts. These were mostly religious works, books of prayer, and explanations of the Bible. Manuscripts were very expensive because of the time they took to produce and the materials used to make them, such as **parchment**. Only the wealthiest people, such as **nobles**, and institutions, including churches and universities, could afford them.

Books were originally handwritten by monks, then, as the demand for books grew, by professional scribes and illustrators. A single book could take years to make, depending on its size.

vne des haultes œuure du noble Charlemaine roy de fran

De plusieurs batailles que Charlemaine eut alenœntre

Some manuscripts, were illuminated, or shone, with illustrations and initial letters painted in gold and silver. These manuscripts, known as illuminated manuscripts, were considered works of art.

First Printing Presses

Copying books by hand was a lot of work. The ancient Chinese discovered that carving a text into wooden blocks and using the blocks to make many copies saved time and effort. The first books in Europe were printed using the same woodblock technology. In the 1450s, Johannes Gutenberg changed the way books were printed by perfecting movable metal type.

Block Printing

Printing was invented in China between 500 A.D. and 700 A.D. It allowed multiple copies of documents, such as government records and contracts, to be made. The Chinese printing press worked like a stamp and ink pad. Each page of a book was carved into a block of wood. All the letters and pictures were carved backward so that they printed the correct way. The woodblocks were rubbed with ink, then the printer put a piece of paper on top of them. The printer rubbed or pressed down on the back of the paper, creating a printed image. The raised parts of the wooden block were the parts that printed. The woodblocks were saved to print more copies.

The first known printed text the same length as a book was the Diamond Sutra, which contained Buddhist teachings. It was printed in China in 868 A.D. by Wang Chieh, on paper in scroll form.

Woodblocks in Europe

In the late 1300s, Europeans printed short texts or small pictures using woodblocks. They pressed the inked woodblocks against paper with their hands, or used an olive or wine press. These presses had been used for centuries to press oil from olives to make olive oil, and to crush grapes for wine.

Johannes Gutenberg

In the 1440s, a metalworker from Germany named Johannes Gutenberg built a press designed specifically for printing books. Like olive and wine presses, Gutenberg's machine used a large wooden screw press to press the paper onto the image that was to be printed. The page was put together with movable type — individual letters, numbers, punctuation marks, and spaces that were arranged to form words and numbers. The type was then rearranged to make a new page.

Johannes Gutenberg developed the printing press so that books could be made faster and more cheaply than by hand.

Metal Movable Type

The movable type that Gutenberg invented was made of metal. He poured liquid metal into molds that contained a matrix, or character stamped into a piece of metal. Then, when he released a spring, the mold loosened and the piece of type fell out. A different matrix was used for each letter of the alphabet, number, and punctuation mark. Gutenberg's methods made producing type faster and easier, and each piece of type looked like others of the same kind, so the letters were easier to read. Gutenberg's metal movable type was used to print books from 1454 to the end of the 1900s.

In the 1040s, Pi Sheng made movable type from pottery, or baked clay.

Preparing to Print

Gutenberg began printing a large edition of the Bible in the early 1450s. While printing on Gutenberg's press was much faster than copying books by hand, the process of printing was still a lot of work. First, a person called a compositor gathered the pieces of type for each line of text. The type was kept in large cases. Capital letters were kept in the upper case and small letters were kept in the lower case. That is why capital letters are called "uppercase letters" and small letters are called "lowercase letters."

Typefaces

Most people today find it difficult to read books printed by Gutenberg's press, or any book printed in the 1400s. Gutenberg based the shapes of letters in his first set of type on people's handwriting at the time, which was very different from handwriting today. Over the next 600 years, new typefaces, or sizes and styles of type, were created that did not resemble handwriting as much and were easier to read. Some typefaces were created for specific purposes. In 1692, King Louis XIV of France ordered a new typeface that only the royal printer could use. He refused to let anyone else even see the matrices! Today, there are thousands of different typefaces.

Only 48 of the 180 Bibles that Gutenberg printed survive. Today, a complete copy is worth nearly 50 million dollars.

Preparing the Page

The compositor set the type in a small wooden tray called a composing stick. It took more than eight hours to set a page of type for Gutenberg's Bible. Once the composing stick was full, the compositor moved the lines of text to a larger tray called a galley, which held a whole page. Galleys were moved to a large table. A rectangular iron frame, called a chase, was placed around several typeset pages. Wooden blocks, called furniture, were fitted into the empty spaces. Sets of wedges, called quoins, were used to squeeze the furniture and letters tight, keeping them from moving. The finished product, called the forme, was placed on the press.

Screw
Platen
Bed of
press

Printing presses modeled after Gutenberg's design were used until 1800.

Two printers could print more than 125 pages in one hour.

Working the Press

It took two printers to work a wooden screw press. One printer, known as the puller, placed a piece of paper in a frame that folded down onto the forme. The other printer, who was called the beater, applied ink to the type using ink balls, which were two large leather pads stuffed with wool. The ink was made from a mixture of boiled plant oils and soot.

A printer turned a wheel to slide the forme under the platen, which was a solid block of wood. Then, he pulled a bar to turn the screw. This lowered the platen, until the paper was sandwiched between the platen and the inked forme. Only half a forme could be printed with one pull, so the printer had to repeat the process for the second half. The printed page was lifted off the forme and hung to dry. Once the page was dry, it was printed on the other side. The first printing presses could only print one color at a time. A page that needed more than one color had to go through the press once for each color.

After Printing

Making a book did not end when the printed pages were lifted off Gutenberg's press and other early presses. Craftsmen known as binders bound books, or attached the pages together inside a cover, and artists and illuminators decorated them with beautiful illustrations.

Binding

Books were sold as folded sheets of paper known as gatherings or quires. Binding a book was usually the responsibility of the person who bought it. Binding books was expensive, and booksellers did not want to spend money on binding books that might not sell.

Books were bound by first stitching the pages together with a needle and thread along one side of the fold. Binders trimmed a book's pages so they were the same size as one another, to produce a clean edge. The front and back covers were stitched on with heavier thread, and secured with a leather cord nailed or screwed into the covers. The first printed books were bound with heavy front and back covers made of solid wood. The wood was then covered with leather. Later covers were made of cardboard covered in leather.

Designs on Bindings

In addition to binding books, binders decorated them. They **impressed** beautiful designs, such as flowers and vines, into the leather covers and spines. The designs were often made with gold leaf, or bits of gold hammered out into very thin sheets. Some books had jewels on their covers, and many covers were engraved with a family's **coat of arms** so that owners could show others that the books were theirs and that they could afford to decorate them beautifully.

In this woodcut of a book binding shop, one binder sews pages together, while the other attaches front and back covers.

Adding Decorations

Until color printing became common in the late 1800s, books were usually printed in black and white. Some book owners wanted their printed books to be as beautiful as medieval illuminated manuscripts, so they hired illuminators to draw fancy capital letters at the beginnings of chapters, and to add gold leaf and color to the pictures. Illuminators also added color borders of leaves and flowers around the pages, and sometimes they added pictures.

Like illuminated manuscripts, beautifully decorated books were often bought by nobles as pieces of art and were displayed prominently in their homes.

Binding Books Today

Books today are bound the same way they were in the 1500s, although some of the materials and tools have changed. The covers of hardcover books are made from cardboard. The pages and covers are sewn together either by hand or by a stitching machine. Most books today are paperbacks. Paperbacks have covers made of stiff, heavy paper. Paperbacks cost less to make and to buy because they are held together by glue rather than stitching.

The coat of arms of Lorenzo de Medici, who was a member of one of the wealthiest and most powerful Italian families in the late 1400s, appears at the bottom of this illuminated page.

Printing Pictures

By the 1490s, a variety of books, as well as newssheets called broadsheets, advertisements, and song sheets, were being printed in Europe. Many printed materials had pictures. At this time, usually only wealthier people knew how to read. With pictures, those who did not know how to read could still learn from and enjoy books.

Woodcuts

The first printed images in Europe were woodcuts. Woodcuts are images carved into blocks of wood, as in earlier block printing. Images are first drawn on wood blocks, then a chisel or knife is used to remove the areas around the lines of the images. The parts in relief, or the areas that are raised, are printed.

Woodcuts were printed on screw presses the same way as text. Many were printed in black and white and colored by hand, while others were printed in color. The first colored woodcut was printed in 1457 in a German Psalter, a book containing the religious hymns and songs from the Bible known as Psalms.

Engravings

An engraving is a picture that is scratched into a flat piece of metal, such as copper, with a sharp tool called a burin. Printing from engravings, where images are below the surface of plates instead of raised above them, is called intaglio printing. With intaglio printing, ink is carefully rubbed into the lines of an engraving. Any ink on the surface of the plate is wiped off so that only the lines of the image will show up and the image will not appear smudged. Printers had to apply a lot of pressure to the paper to pick up the ink below the plate's surface, so special presses were used to print engravings.

Woodcuts were used until the 1850s in many different types of printed materials, including books, newspapers, and advertising posters. This woodcut, from 1490, taught children the Latin alphabet.

(left) Artists often included more details in engravings than in woodcuts, since copper is easier to carve than wood. Like most engravings, this one from an atlas was printed in black and white and was colored by hand.

(below) To print multi-colored lithographic images, such as this advertisement for a theater performance, printers used a different stone for each color, or they reused the same stone, cleaning it off and redrawing each new part of the image in a new color.

Lithographs

Lithography was invented by Alois Senefelder in Germany around 1798, and is based on the chemical principle that grease and water do not mix. Senefelder drew images using a greasy ink or pencil on a piece of limestone, and then poured water over the stone. The water was absorbed by the limestone where there was no ink. When Senefelder covered the stone with normal printing ink, the ink stuck only to the area with the image, because the wet parts **repelled** the ink. Like a printing plate, the stone was then put through a special press that moved over the surface of the stone, and the image was printed. Lithography is now the most common technique used to print both text and images.

E. T. SMITH'S
GRAND PANTOMIME

JACK AND THE BEAN STALK

ASTLEY'S ROYAL AMPHITHEATRE
OPEN EVERY EVENING—REDUCED PRICES

Changing Lives

Before the printing press, few books were available and few people could afford them. Slowly, from the 1450s onward, books became less expensive, although they were still not affordable enough for everyone. Many people who lived in small villages owned only one book, usually a copy of the Bible or a prayer book, or no books at all.

Broadsheets

By the 1600s, printed items, including books, newspapers, maps, and broadsheets, were everywhere. Broadsheets were one-page sheets that included text and woodcut pictures. Some broadsheets spread news, others advertised products and events, while still others were for entertainment. They were posted in public places, such as taverns and churches, sold on street corners, or rented out from bookstores. Modern newspapers developed from broadsheets. The first English daily newspaper appeared in London in 1702.

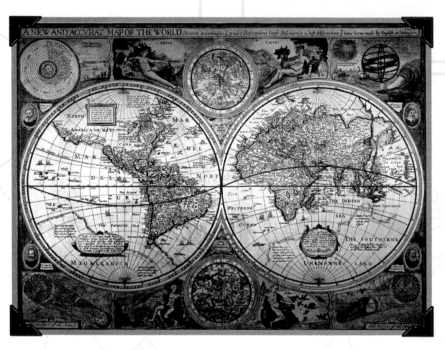

Once printed maps became common, more people became aware of the size of their country and what the world looked like.

New Kinds of Books

Before the printing press, most books in Europe were about religion and were made for **clergy**, **scholars**, and nobles. The printing press made publishing books much less expensive, and new types of books for information and entertainment started to appear. In 1602, the French printer Nicolas Oudot began to publish books with used type, reused woodcuts, and inexpensive paper. The books, which included novels, plays, children's books, and travel adventure stories, cost little to buy and were extremely popular. They were bound in blue paper, and became known as the "Blue Library."

Working with Books

Before Johannes Gutenberg, 20,000 to 30,000 books existed in Europe. By 1500, that number had risen to between 8 and 24 million. With more books being printed, the number of people involved in book production grew. More people became booksellers, papermakers, illustrators, and book binders. In large cities and small towns, bookstores became meeting places, where people discussed the news and formed reading groups to talk about the books they read.

(right) In The Starry Messenger, *published in 1610, the astronomer Galileo Galilei described and drew pictures of the things he saw in space with his telescope, including the very first images of the Moon's craters and mountains.*

Reactions against the Press

Not everyone thought the printing press was a great invention. At first, many of the wealthiest people refused to buy printed books because they did not consider them as valuable or as beautiful as books written by hand. Church officials worried that, with so many books available, people might read about ideas that the Church disagreed with. The Church worried these ideas could spread quickly and disrupt society.

(left) Books that governments or the Church did not approve of were sometimes burned in public places as a warning to people not to buy or read them.

More Words

From the 1450s to 1800, only minor changes were made to the printing press. For example, iron screws replaced wooden ones, so that platens could be pressed onto formes with greater force. Many more improvements were made between 1800 and 1960. These sped up the printing process and made printers' jobs easier.

The Stanhope Press

In the 1800s and 1900s, every major improvement to the printing press resulted from the demands of newspaper printing. Newspaper publishers must print many copies of a newspaper in a very short time, so they are always looking for faster and less expensive printing methods. In 1800, English inventor Earl Charles Stanhope designed the Stanhope press, the first press made entirely of iron. Iron is much stronger than wood, so the Stanhope press could push paper against type with greater force.

The Stanhope press had a larger platen than Gutenberg's press, so a page could be printed with one pull of the bar that lowered the platen instead of two pulls. This saved time.

The Columbian Press

The Columbian press was invented by George Clymer of Philadelphia around 1813. Like the Stanhope press, it was made completely of iron, but instead of using a screw to lower the platen, it used levers and a **piston**, with a series of **counterweights**. This lever design increased the amount of force with which the platen could be pressed down onto the forme. A printer using a Columbian press needed even less physical strength than a printer using a Stanhope press.

The Cylinder Press

In 1811, Friedrich Koenig, a German living in London, built the first working press powered by steam. Steam power moved the parts of the press, so a printer's strength was no longer required to print a page. Koenig's press was known as a cylinder press. The bed of the press, which was the flat part that held the forme, was always moving. First, it passed under ink rollers, which applied ink to the forme. Then, the forme moved under a cylinder wrapped in a sheet of paper, called the impression cylinder. The impression cylinder rolled on top of the forme to print the page.

In 1818, Koenig designed a double press. Once a sheet of paper was printed on one side, it was automatically passed to another cylinder that printed the other side. This saved time and money, since a sheet of paper did not have to be put through the press twice to print on both sides.

(right) With the cylinder press, paper did not have to be fed into the machine as single sheets.

(above) Large Columbian presses were used to print books and newspapers, while smaller Columbian presses were used to print newsletters, invitations, and personalized stationary.

The Rotary Press

In the 1840s, American inventor Richard Hoe invented the rotary press. Like Koenig's press, Hoe's press was made of cylinders and was powered by steam, but it had no bed. Instead, curved type plates were attached to a cylinder. Ink rollers applied ink to the type plates, then the ink-covered type rolled against the paper. Printing in more than one color was much faster, easier, and less expensive with the rotary press. A multicolored page only had to go through the press once, passing under different plates and ink cylinders for each color.

TEN CYLINDER TYPE-REVOLVING PRINTING MACHINE.

The Web Press

In 1865, an American named William Bullock made the first roll-fed rotary press. It worked like Hoe's cylinder press, except a large roll of paper was hooked to a reel at the end of the press. As the pages printed, the paper unrolled to provide the press with a constant supply of paper. There was no need to insert single sheets of paper, and the paper did not have to be removed for the other side to print. Bullock's press was named the "web press" because the way the paper moved as it was fed into the press reminded people of a spider spinning a web. Bullock's press could print 10,000 doubled-sided sheets an hour.

The first rotary press printed up to 8,000 sheets an hour. A press like this one had several sets of cylinders and paper feeding stations, allowing more than one copy of a page to be printed at a time. Newspapers could be printed even faster.

700	**1300**	**1455**	**1798**	**1800**	**1811**
The first printing presses are used in China.	The first cloth paper mills are operating in Europe.	Johannes Gutenberg finishes printing the first book in Europe using his wooden screw press and movable metal type.	Alois Senefelder invents the process of lithography.	Charles Stanhope invents a metal press, known as the Stanhope Press.	Friedrich Koenig invents the cylinder press, the first steam-powered printing press.

Changes in Typesetting

Setting the type one piece at a time was the longest part of the printing process. In 1886, German-born American Ottmar Mergenthaler invented a machine called a Linotype to set type. An operator used a keyboard, similar to today's computer keyboards, to input lines of text. Then, the Linotype cast the text in lines of molten lead at 535° Fahrenheit (280° Celsius). The lines of type were then assembled into pages to be printed on the press. A later invention called the Monotype cast metal type in separate pieces instead of in lines. This was useful when different kinds of characters, such as italic letters or mathematical symbols, were needed on a line or page.

Phototypesetting

Phototypesetting was invented in the 1950s. It became very common in the 1970s, when it replaced Linotype typesetting in most newspaper and printing shops. Phototypesetting is called "cold type" because it does not use molten metal to make pieces of type or plates. Instead, the text is typed onto high-quality paper and then photographed to produce a sheet of film. The film is developed onto a light-sensitive aluminum printing plate. Phototypesetting is a faster form of typesetting. It is also less expensive than other methods of setting type because it uses less metal.

Linotype operators could set 14 lines of newspaper text each minute. A single linotype operator was able to perform the work of six or seven hand compositors.

1812	1840s	1886	1904	1950s	1997	2000
George Clymer uses a new lever and piston design in his Columbian press.	Richard Hoe invents the rotary press, a press that made printing in color easier.	Ottmar Mergenthaler invents the Linotype, an automated machine that sets type.	Ira Rubel builds the first offset printing press to print newspapers.	The invention of phototypesetting makes typesetting faster and less expensive.	*The New York Times* begins to use computers in each step of the printing process.	Digital offset presses become more common.

Parts of a Press

Today, all newspapers and most books are printed on a type of rotary press called a lithographic offset press. The first offset printing press was built in 1904 by American Ira W. Rubel. "Offset" refers to the fact that the printing plate never touches the paper. Offset printing presses are powered by electricity, which replaced steam as a source of power in the 1920s.

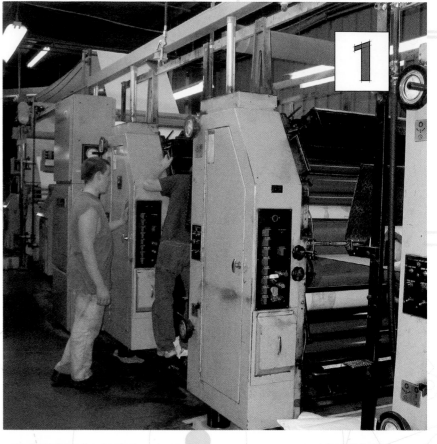

1. Web press: Paper flows through the printing units where different colored inks are layered one on top of each other. Each unit contains one of the main process colors, magenta, cyan, yellow, and black. These colors combine to form all other colors. This press can print both sides of a page at the same time.

2. Paper reel: Paper on a massive reel is fed into the press as a continuous roll. The paper follows a path that leads up and down through the machine in a web-like fashion.

3. Ink rollers: Ink rollers spread greasy ink over the part of the plate with the image. The ink rolls off the parts of the plate where the water has sunk in.

4. Plate cylinder: The text and pictures that will be printed are created from computer files and transferred onto thin metal plates. The plate cylinder holds these prepared plates. When printing in more than one color, separate printing plates are usually made for black, magenta, cyan, and yellow.

Water rollers (not shown): These rollers wet the printing plate and wash ink off of areas of the plates that do not contain images or text.

5. Blanket cylinder: The plate cylinder presses against the blanket cylinder, which is covered by a sheet of rubber. The image of the page to be printed is transferred to the rubber sheet. Since the plates never touch the paper, they do not wear down or break as quickly as plates used on other types of presses. This is the part of the process where the actual printing occurs.

Feeding the Press

Since the ancient Egyptians, people have used different materials, including plants, animal skins, and cloth, to create writing surfaces. As printing became more common, people had to develop a writing surface that was easy to make, durable, and inexpensive.

Papyrus

Papyrus is a marsh plant that was used in Egypt to make the first paper-like surface around 3000 B.C. The word "paper" comes from this plant's name. To make papyrus, the inner strips of the plant's stem were removed, beaten, and woven together. The sap inside acted like glue, holding the strips together.

(above) Papyrus was fragile, and pages that were handled a lot often fell apart. The paper's surface was also very rough, which made it difficult to write on with fine lines.

Parchment

By 200 A.D. in Europe, a new material, called parchment, had replaced papyrus. Parchment is made from animal pelt, or an animal's thick, hairy outer skin. Sheep, cattle, and goat pelts were the most common. The animal pelts were soaked in a mixture of water and **lime** for about a week, then stretched out on a large wooden frame to dry. The parchment maker used a curved knife to scrape off any remaining hair and thin the skin. Then, he used a stone called pumice to polish the skin, and rubbed the skin with chalk until the parchment was smooth, thin, and pale enough to write on.

(left) Parchment lasted for a very long time without breaking or absorbing all of the ink, so that words and images did not fade.

Cloth Paper

The oldest piece of cloth paper still in existence was made in China around 100 B.C. Europeans started making paper from cloth in the 1100s. Linen rags made from the strong fibers of the flax plant were left soaking in a tub of water for many days. Once the rags dissolved into a runny, lumpy pulp, the papermaker placed a wire frame the same size and shape as a piece of paper into the tub and scooped out pulp. The papermaker dumped the sheet of pulp onto a sheet of felt, repeating the process several times. Then, the pulp and felt stack was squeezed in a press to remove the water, and the sheets of paper were hung to dry. The dried sheets were dipped in glue, a process called sizing, so that ink would not soak into the paper too much.

This image from the late 1500s shows a cloth papermaker at work, placing a wire frame into a tub of pulp.

With forests disappearing, it is more difficult and expensive for papermaking factories to get trees.

Wood Pulp Paper

In Germany in the 1840s, printers and papermakers began to use chips of wood, which were less expensive than cloth, to make paper. Wood paper was made the same way as cloth paper, but papermakers beat the wood with mallets as it was soaking to help break it down into pulp. In the 1870s, chemicals made the process much faster.

Today, paper is made in large factories with many papermaking machines. So much wood is being used to make paper and other products that forests all over the world are disappearing. Now, most books and newspapers are printed on recycled paper. Recycled paper is made partly from new materials and partly from used paper and paper products that are shredded and cleaned with chemicals.

Using Computers

The biggest change to the printing press was the invention and development of the computer. Computers are used in many stages of the printing process, both on the press and off. This makes the printing process easier, faster, and less expensive.

Computer Typesetting

The invention of typesetting machines in the late 1800s and phototypesetting in the 1950s made composing a printed page much faster and easier than composing by hand. Today, all composition is done on computers. People use computers to write and edit texts, and to arrange and design every part of every page. Once the look of a page is finalized, the compositor transfers the page to a special computer that prints it as a printing plate, ready to be put on the press. Composing and preparing printing plates, the most time-consuming parts of the printing process, are no longer necessary.

Now that composition is done on computers, compositors can change the look of a page by moving blocks of text, images, page numbers, and borders with only a few clicks of a mouse.

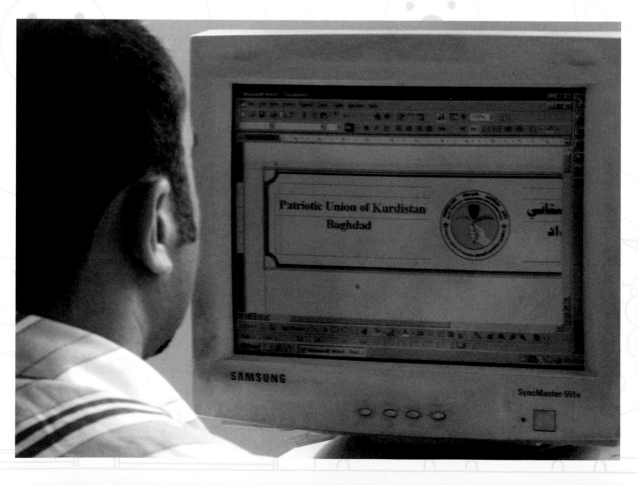

Computers on the Press

Computers control the release of inks to the ink rollers, the amount of paper that goes into the press, and the speed of printing. On some presses, computers allow pages to be entered in and stored long before they are printed, reducing the work that press workers must do at the time of printing. This feature is especially important for newspapers that print large weekend editions. It allows them to prepare sections that do not contain breaking news, such as book reviews or home sections, in advance.

Going Digital

In digital printing, words and images are transferred from a computer screen to a digital printer, such as a laser printer. Digital printers are usually used when a small number of copies must be printed quickly. There are no plates to prepare, so setting up for printing does not take very long.

With digital printing, it is also easy to make changes to a page by editing it on the computer and printing it again. This is useful when someone notices a mistake, or when a person is printing similar documents one after the other, for example, envelopes and invitations with different names and addresses.

With presses controlled by computers, it is easy to print extra copies of books because all the information needed for printing is stored in the computer.

Digital printers use an electrical charge to transfer powdered or liquid ink to paper or cardboard.

Print in Daily Life

The products of the printing press are everywhere. In addition to books and newspapers, printing presses are used to make calendars, posters, billboards, and food packaging, and to print designs on wallpaper and linoleum tiles. Some items are created using specialized printing presses, while others use different kinds of paper and ink.

Books

A book is printed somewhere in the world every 30 seconds. Books are printed for adults and children on almost every subject imaginable, including dinosaurs, volcanoes, car repair, gardening, and travel.

Many people work in the book industry. Some people write, edit, or print books, while others design, bind, and sell them. Until the late 1800s, the same person did many of these jobs. Printers often printed books on presses in the backs of buildings, and sold them in stores at the front. Today, printing houses are mainly responsible for running the presses. Deciding what books should be written, working with authors to develop books, and deciding what books will look like is the responsibility of publishing houses.

One of a printer's jobs is to check the colors of book covers to make sure they are crisp, clear, and not smudged.

Presses run until the early hours of the morning, printing newspapers that will be delivered to newsstands and people's homes just a few hours later.

Newspapers

There are more than 60,000 newspapers in the world, including 8,000 that are published daily. Newspapers provide information on politics, sports, science, business, and entertainment, as well as crossword puzzles, advertisements, movie reviews, and much more.

Offset presses used to print newspapers usually print much faster than other presses since newspapers must print many pages in a short time. Some of the fastest computerized printing presses in the world are in New Jersey, at the printer of *The New York Times*. In one hour, each press can print 72,000 copies of a 160-page color newspaper.

Censorship

The governments of some countries review books and other materials before they are made available to the public. If they feel that the materials contain ideas and opinions with which they disagree, they censor, or do not allow, them to be printed or sold. Many authors and printers have been fined, jailed, threatened with death, or even killed for writing and printing books against their governments' wishes.

The very popular Harry Potter books, by British author J.K. Rowling, have been banned in some school libraries in North America. Some people believe that the books are dangerous for children because they are about magic.

Catalogs

Catalogs are books or magazines that list products for sale, with a picture, description, and price of each item. Some catalogs use a special type of printing called rotogravure. Text and images in rotogravure printing are engraved, using computers and laser beam machines, on cylinder-shaped copper plates. The plates are then inked and the images are printed. Rotogravure presses, which are a type of rotary press, transfer more ink to the paper than other presses, and the computer laser technology produces very detailed pictures.

(above) Rotogravure presses produce pictures of a very high quality. This is why rotogravure printing is more expensive than other types of printing.

Wishing You Well

In 1843, American J.C. Horsley designed and printed the first Christmas card for a friend. The idea of greeting cards, as well as the greeting card industry, grew out of Horsley's Christmas card. Today, cards for different occasions express wishes such as "Happy birthday," "Congratulations," and "Get well soon."

(left) J.C. Horsley's Christmas card is a lithograph. In the 1800s, lithography made printing images in color much simpler than any other printing method.

Hello from Far Away

In 1870, the French army printed the first picture postcard. The army thought that it would be easier for soldiers to write quick notes to their families on the backs of postcards than to write letters. Shortly after, postcards were made for ordinary people who were on holiday in other cities so that they could send short messages to friends and family back home. Today, millions of greeting cards and postcards are sent around the world every year. All are printed on specialized presses designed for printing a lot of different colors and images, with bits of black and white text.

In the late 1800s and early 1900s, some postcards showed people using a new invention, the telephone.

The American Treasury Department is one of the busiest printing facilities in the world, printing more than 37 million currency notes a day.

Money

Money, in the form of bills or notes, is one of the most commonly used items printed on the printing press. Bills are printed on a special kind of cloth paper using the intaglio process, like engravings. A master engraver carefully produces the image of the bill on a steel printing plate by hand. The presses used to print money apply so much pressure to the paper that the ink on bills is slightly raised off the paper. No other printing press or technique produces this effect.

Different techniques are used to make it difficult for people to produce counterfeit, or fake, money. In the United States, the ink used to print real money contains tiny, metallic flakes that reflect light. Bills that are tilted back and forth appear to change color. Small red and blue threads, which can be seen when a bill is examined closely, are also added to the pulp used to make the cloth paper.

Future of Printing

As they have throughout history, printers continue to look for ways to increase the speed and decrease the costs of printing. They are also trying to make printing less harmful to the environment by experimenting with different chemicals used in the printing process and with new methods for making paper.

The Latest in Printing Presses

Printing presses today rely more and more on computers to manage the printing process. Computers help operators monitor the quality of pages as they print, identifying pages that are crumpled or missing ink. Computers also allow printers to set up a press for the next job while it is completing the current job, reducing preparation time.

Printers are experimenting with digital offset printing presses, called direct imaging presses. The computer files of each page are transferred directly to the press, which then makes plates ready to be printed. Changes can be made to a page until the moment the page is sent to the press.

Changes in Paper

Today, the recycled content of paper is higher than before. This means that fewer trees are needed to make paper, helping conserve forests. Papermakers and printers are also trying to protect the environment by recycling waste from the papermaking process. Some of the waste created when wood and used paper are broken down into pulp is made into other substances. For example, bark and wood chips are made into fertilizers.

Millions of pieces of paper and paper products enter recycling plants every day.

In 2006, Chen Chia-Chun, from China, invented a new type of printing called "Flash Paper." Special photographic paper is placed on a computer screen, and the image on the screen "prints," or is transferred, onto the paper without a printing press.

(below) The Compaq iPAQ 3630 is a handheld computer on which two dozen e-books can be downloaded.

No Need for the Printing Press?

Some people wonder if, one day, printing presses will no longer be necessary. "Talking books," or books read aloud by authors or actors, are available on CDs or can be downloaded to computers. Encyclopedias, dictionaries, and atlases are available on CD-ROMs or on the World Wide Web. Books and magazines, called e-books and e-zines, are now published on websites, as are many newspapers. People e-mail digital greeting cards to each other, and companies advertise online. Since materials published digitally do not use paper, they are better for the environment.

In the 1450s, many people could not understand why someone would prefer a printed book over a manuscript book. Today, many people feel the same way about e-books. As long as people still want to buy printed books, both technologies will exist side by side.

Glossary

astronomer A person who studies the stars, planets, and moons

Buddhist Relating to Buddhism, a religion that began in India and that is based on the teachings of the Buddha

clergy Religious officials

coat of arms A design that is used by a particular family as its symbol

counterweight A weight or force that balances another

impress To make a mark on a surface by applying pressure

Latin The language of the ancient Romans and the Roman Catholic Church

lime A white powdery substance that is made by heating limestone or shells

Middle Ages The period from about 500 A.D. to 1500 A.D. in western Europe

monk A male member of a religious community who devotes his life to prayer, work, and study

noble A member of a ruling class

parchment A material made from animal skin on which people write

piston A cylinder that slides up and down inside a larger cylinder under the pressure of steam or hot gases

repel To push or force something away

scholar A learned person

scribe A person who writes out or copies documents and manuscripts

soot A back powder produced from burning oil, wood, or coal

stylus A piece of bone, ivory, or metal with a very sharp point, used for writing

Index

Printed in the U.S.A.